THE VIKING CODEX

THE SAGA OF LEIF ERIKSSON

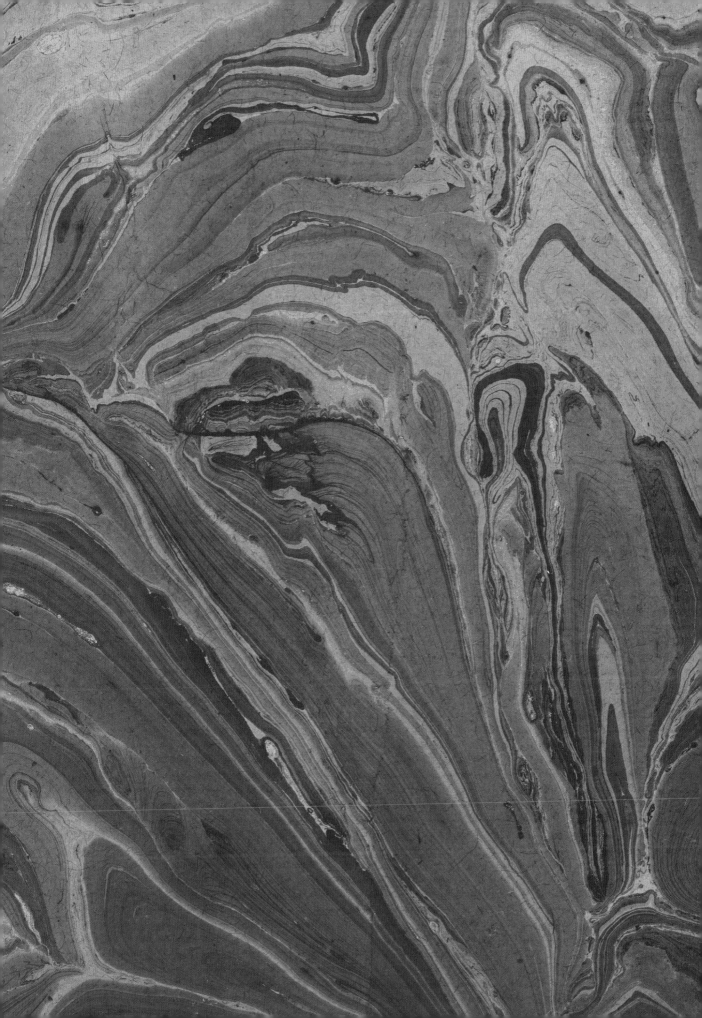

CONTENTS

Published in Great Britain in 2008 by
Book House, an imprint of
The Salariya Book Company Ltd
25 Marlborough Place, Brighton BN1 1UB
www.salariya.com
www.book-house.co.uk

SALARIYA

1 3 5 7 9 8 6 4 2

A CIP catalogue record for this book is available
from the British Library.

Printed and bound in China.
Printed on paper from sustainable sources.

HB ISBN-13: 978-1-906370-61-9
PB ISBN-13: 978-1-906370-62-6

Created and designed by: David Salariya
Editorial Assistant: Mark Williams

Visit our website at **www.salariya.com**
for **free** electronic versions of:
You Wouldn't Want to be an Egyptian Mummy!
You Wouldn't Want to be a Roman Gladiator!
Avoid Joining Shackleton's Polar Expedition!
Avoid Sailing on a 19th-Century Whaling Ship!

THE VIKING CODEX

THE SAGA OF LEIF ERIKSSON

FIONA MACDONALD
ILLUSTRATED BY MARK BERGIN

INTRODUCTION

Like father, like son! This book tells the story of two great Viking explorers: Erik the Red and his son, Leif the Lucky. They led sailors and settlers across the wild Atlantic Ocean to new homes in faraway lands.

Erik was born in Norway around AD 940. But his family had to leave quickly, in disgrace, 'because of some killings'.

They escaped to Iceland, where their bold, brave and bad behaviour was remembered by Icelandic storytellers long after they had died. Around AD 1200, their adventures were written down in sagas (exciting epics), and so have survived until today. Read on, and find out more!

AT HOME IN ICELAND

Freeman: rich trader

Earl: noble chieftain and war leader

Soon after AD 800, fierce Viking fighting men and peaceful farming families began to sail away from Scandinavia to make new homes overseas. They went in search of land – and to find freedom from newly powerful kings. The first Viking settlers reached Iceland around AD 870. By AD 930, over 30,000 Viking men, women and children lived there.

Slave: foreigner, captured in a raid

Freeman: poor farmer or craftworker

VIKING LANDS

Viking migrants settled over a vast area, from Russia to southern Italy. Viking merchants ventured still further, to trade in Baghdad and Constantinople (now Istanbul).

Constantinople

Baghdad

NOBLES, FREE PEOPLE, SLAVES

Vikings were not all equal. Free people might be rich or poor, but they had the right to own land and weapons – and the duty to fight for their earl. Slaves belonged to their owners, and had few possessions, but they could buy their freedom or be set free.

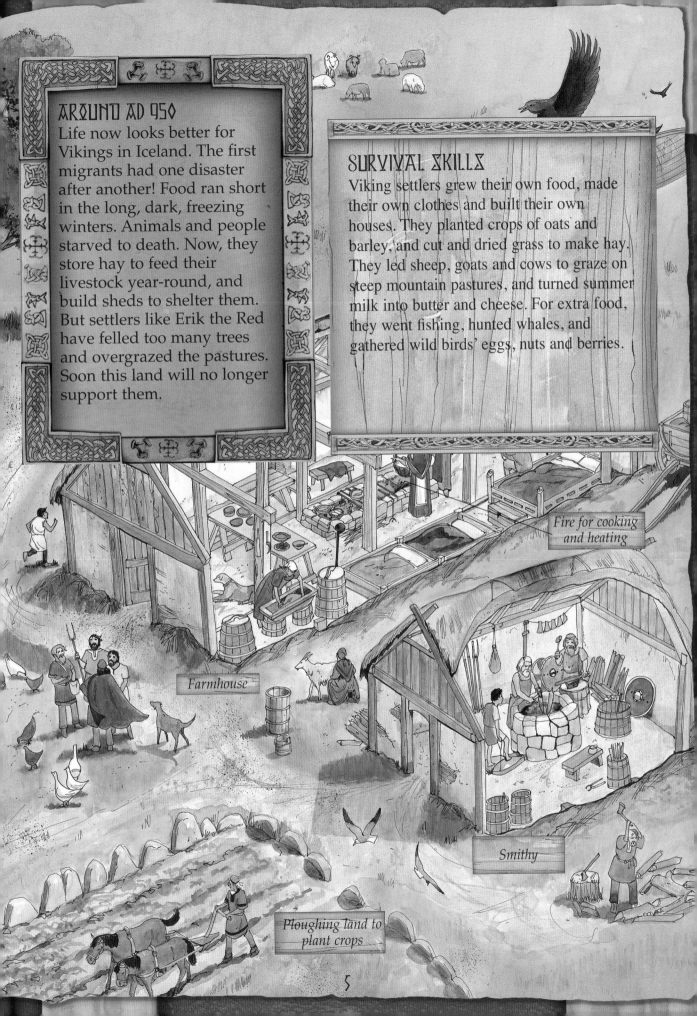

AROUND AD 950

Life now looks better for Vikings in Iceland. The first migrants had one disaster after another! Food ran short in the long, dark, freezing winters. Animals and people starved to death. Now, they store hay to feed their livestock year-round, and build sheds to shelter them. But settlers like Erik the Red have felled too many trees and overgrazed the pastures. Soon this land will no longer support them.

SURVIVAL SKILLS

Viking settlers grew their own food, made their own clothes and built their own houses. They planted crops of oats and barley, and cut and dried grass to make hay. They led sheep, goats and cows to graze on steep mountain pastures, and turned summer milk into butter and cheese. For extra food, they went fishing, hunted whales, and gathered wild birds' eggs, nuts and berries.

Fire for cooking and heating

Farmhouse

Smithy

Ploughing land to plant crops

5

RAIDERS AND TRADERS

In Iceland, settlers grabbed as much land as they could, hoping to grow rich and powerful. But Vikings also sought wealth in other ways – by raiding and trading. Tough Viking pirates terrorised peaceful villages and monasteries, snatching treasure and seizing captives. Shrewd Viking traders travelled to fairs and markets, selling rare, valuable goods and everyday essentials.

Sudden, deadly attacks! Viking raiders swooped in from the sea to attack coastal communities throughout Europe. A single lucky raid might make a Viking warrior rich for life!

WONDERFUL THINGS

Archaeologists excavating Viking settlements and burials have found treasures made by Viking craftworkers or imported from distant lands. They include silver neck-rings and brooches from Sweden, sharp swords and delicate glass from Germany, necklaces from Russia, and silk, metalwork and coins from the Middle East.

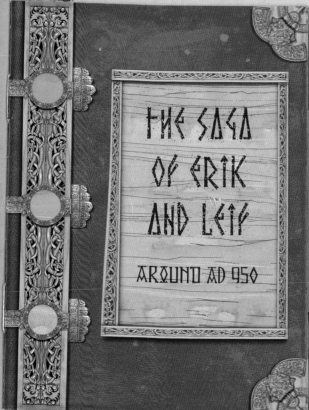

THE SAGA
OF ERIK
AND LEIF

AROUND AD 950

OUTLAW!

Settlers in Iceland brought many Viking laws and customs with them. But they refused to let their new homeland be ruled by kings. They wanted to be free to govern themselves. So, to settle disputes and make laws for their own communities, they organised traditional *Things* (law-courts and assemblies). All free adult men could attend.

A family's honour was immensely important. Wrongdoing by one family member brought shame on all their relations – and often started a long-running, bloody feud.

VIKING JUSTICE

Men accused of crimes were tried at *Thing* meetings. Criminals and victims both brought friends to support them. The man with the most friends (or the most powerful friends) was usually declared innocent. Vikings believed that this was best for the community as a whole. Punishments included fines, execution, or being made an outlaw. An outlawed man had to leave his homeland for three years, or, sometimes, for ever. If he returned, he might be killed.

The Vikings' values grew out of their harsh environment and struggle to survive. They admired toughness, hard work and generosity in both men and women – but were not ashamed to be brutal and ruthless.

Feuding families sought revenge by fighting each other. A feud might end if one family accepted money – or it might continue until all the men of fighting age had been killed.

The Iceland national *Thing* met for a fortnight every summer. Meetings were led by a Law-Speaker and a council of nobles. Laws were not written down, but a third of them were recited out loud each year, so that people would remember them.

Men involved in a quarrel could challenge each other to a duel. The loser was judged to be guilty.

Disputes could be settled peacefully if a wrongdoer agreed to pay his victim a heavy fine.

AROUND AD 972

Oh no! Not again! Hot-tempered Erik the Red has killed another man! Even worse, the murder took place at the yearly meeting of the *Thing* when everyone is meant to be peaceful. Eric bumped into a farmer with whom he had been feuding. They argued and this led to an ugly brawl. Now Erik's enemy is dead! The *Thing* council is furious, and has outlawed Erik.

GREEN AND PLEASANT?

Erik the Red and his companions arrived in Greenland in AD 982. The first Viking settlers there found stark mountains and barren ice-sheets. The shallow soil supported little grass and no trees, but the seas teemed with fish and the cliffs housed huge colonies of seabirds. The settlers hunted seals and polar bears for their skins and fur, killed reindeer and whales for meat and blubber (fat), and walrus for their valuable tusks.

Fish drying in the wind (to preserve them to eat in winter)

Erik the Red built a farmhouse at Brattahlid (now Qagssiarssuk) at the southern tip of Greenland.

Nothing remains of the first Viking homes in Greenland. They were probably similar to this house from Iceland.

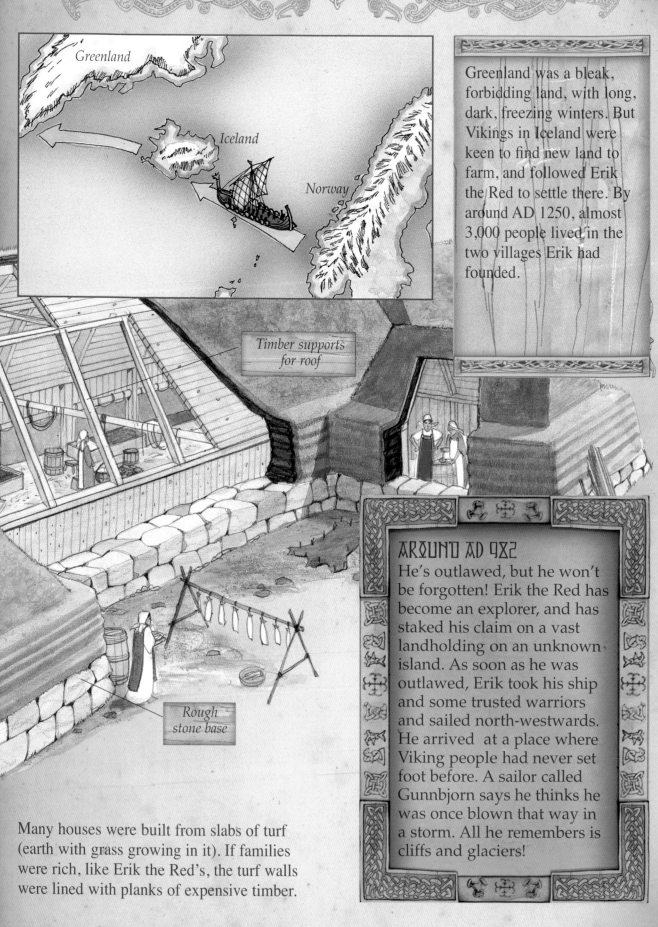

Greenland

Iceland

Norway

Greenland was a bleak, forbidding land, with long, dark, freezing winters. But Vikings in Iceland were keen to find new land to farm, and followed Erik the Red to settle there. By around AD 1250, almost 3,000 people lived in the two villages Erik had founded.

Timber supports for roof

Rough stone base

AROUND AD 982

He's outlawed, but he won't be forgotten! Erik the Red has become an explorer, and has staked his claim on a vast landholding on an unknown island. As soon as he was outlawed, Erik took his ship and some trusted warriors and sailed north-westwards. He arrived at a place where Viking people had never set foot before. A sailor called Gunnbjorn says he thinks he was once blown that way in a storm. All he remembers is cliffs and glaciers!

Many houses were built from slabs of turf (earth with grass growing in it). If families were rich, like Erik the Red's, the turf walls were lined with planks of expensive timber.

FAMILY LIFE

Wherever they lived, Vikings depended on their families. Without family help and loyalty, survival was hard. Family members worked together. Parents taught children all their own skills, as children were expected to be useful. Sickly babies and weak old people who became a burden might be left to die.

THE SAGA
OF ERIK
AND LEIF

AROUND AD 995

Farm tools hung on wooden wall

Father carving wood

Child fetching kindling

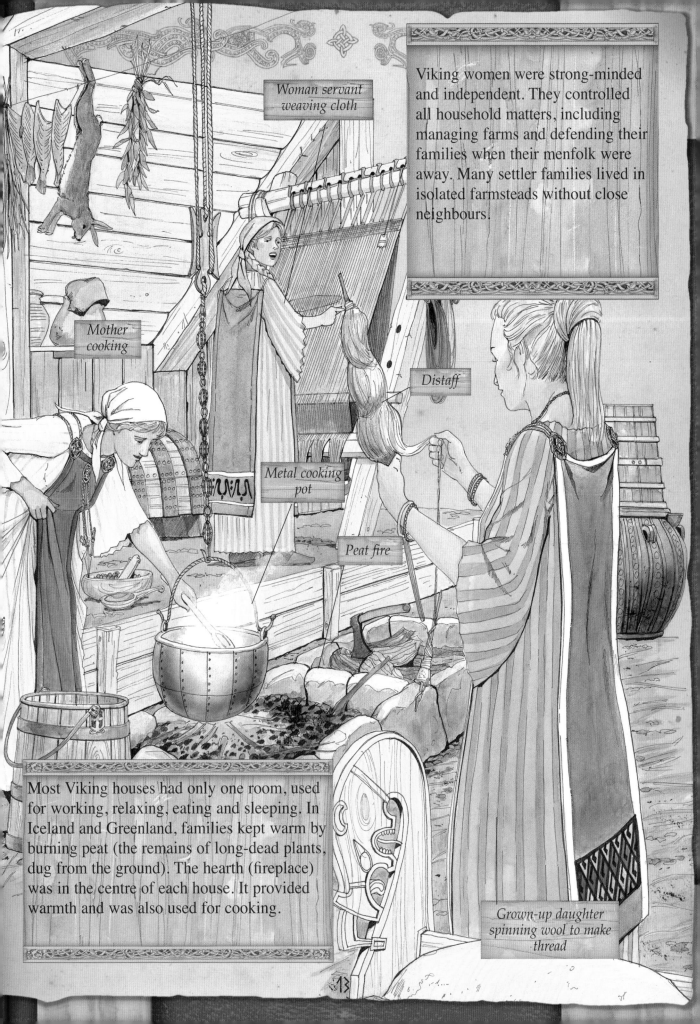

Woman servant
weaving cloth

Viking women were strong-minded
and independent. They controlled
all household matters, including
managing farms and defending their
families when their menfolk were
away. Many settler families lived in
isolated farmsteads without close
neighbours.

Mother
cooking

Distaff

Metal cooking
pot

Peat fire

Most Viking houses had only one room, used
for working, relaxing, eating and sleeping. In
Iceland and Greenland, families kept warm by
burning peat (the remains of long-dead plants,
dug from the ground). The hearth (fireplace)
was in the centre of each house. It provided
warmth and was also used for cooking.

Grown-up daughter
spinning wool to make
thread

SHIPS AND THE SEA

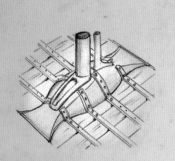

The Vikings were skilful sailors who steered their fast, beautiful ships through the wild, dangerous conditions of the northern seas. From childhood, boys were taught how to row and sail. Viking ships were powered by the wind blowing a single square woollen sail, or by men rowing. They were steered by a large oar at the stern (back).

AROUND AD 997

It must be over two years since I last wrote about Erik the Red and his family. The twenty-five boat loads of settlers that decided to join him from Iceland are still surviving in Greenland. He's had no time for quarrelling or fighting since then. Building and farming keep him busy. But his young son, Leif, seems to have inherited his father's energy and ambition. They say he's a promising sailor, too. That young man may go far one day!

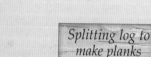

Splitting log to make planks

Wedge

Adze

Out at sea, Vikings steered by observing the stars: the Pole Star shows north, and the sun at its highest point in the sky shows south. Seabirds, drifting plants and animal smells were all signs that land might be near.

Ferry

Knarr
(trading ship)

Longship
(warship)

River boat

Clamps

Strakes

Mallet

DIFFERENT KINDS OF SHIPS

River boats and ferries carried
passengers along rivers and around
coasts. They were small, with shallow
hulls, and were easy to row or sail.
Knarrs (trading ships) had wide,
deep hulls to carry lots of cargo. They
were strongly built for long journeys
through rough seas.
Longships (warships) were designed
for speed. Their narrow, flexible hulls
skimmed rapidly over the waves.

SHIPBUILDING

Viking craftsmen used simple hand-
powered tools to build their ships from
Scandinavian timbers. Oak was used for
ships' keels (backbones) and ribs; decks,
masts and oars were usually made from
pine. Strakes (curved planks) of oak were
tied to the ribs using tough spruce-tree
roots, and held together with iron nails.
Joints were caulked (stuffed) with tarred
wool to keep out water.

The sight of a ship sailing into a sea fjord (narrow bay) caused excitement – and sometimes fear – in any Viking village. Were the sailors friends or foes? peaceful traders or angry enemies? or perhaps long-lost family members?

Viking sailors all had tales to tell about the mishaps and terrors of their voyages. Going to sea was risky. Even the best ships and most skilful sailors could be lost in a freak accident or sudden storm. Viking storytellers also warned how strange sea-monsters – like the Kraken (a giant squid-like creature) or the man-eating Maelstrom (a whirlpool) – could drag sailors down below the waves to their doom.

WINTER WITH THE KING

T he first Vikings were led by noble chiefs, who protected farming families in their neighbourhood. In return, they demanded loyalty. But by AD 900, a few Viking nobles had grown extremely powerful. They turned the lands they controlled into three separate kingdoms: Norway, Sweden and Denmark.

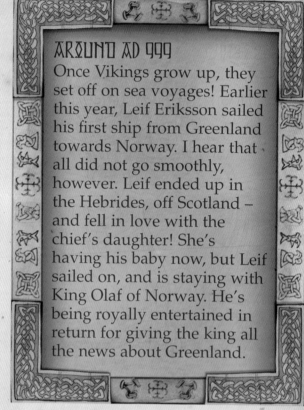

AROUND AD 999

Once Vikings grow up, they set off on sea voyages! Earlier this year, Leif Eriksson sailed his first ship from Greenland towards Norway. I hear that all did not go smoothly, however. Leif ended up in the Hebrides, off Scotland – and fell in love with the chief's daughter! She's having his baby now, but Leif sailed on, and is staying with King Olaf of Norway. He's being royally entertained in return for giving the king all the news about Greenland.

VIKING FEASTS

The Vikings loved parties! Kings and nobles gave feasts to reward their loyal warriors or to welcome honoured guests. Ordinary families held feasts on special days such as midwinter, or to celebrate events like weddings. Food for feasts was as lavish as the host could provide – Vikings believed that generosity was the sign of a noble spirit. There was always plenty of meat, bread and wine or ale. Cheese, nuts, berries, honey and cream might follow.

Woman servant
pouring wine

Skald *singing
a poem*

Guest holding
drinking horn

Skalds (royal poets) sang the praises of
kings and entertained guests visiting
royal halls. Viking poems and stories
were not written down, but memorised
and passed on from father to son.

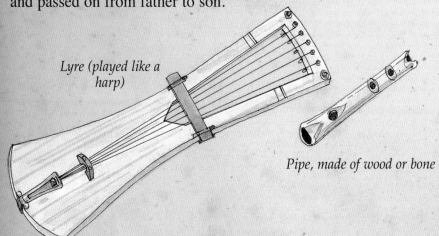

Lyre (played like a
harp)

Pipe, made of wood or bone

11

OLD GODS, NEW CHURCH

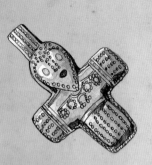

The Vikings believed in many gods and goddesses. Each one watched over a different side of life. Vikings sacrificed animals and people to please the gods and asked for their help and protection.

Vikings liked to wear amulets (lucky charms) shaped like the god Thor's magic hammer.

By around AD 1100, most Vikings had become Christians. But some still believed in the old gods as well.

AROUND AD 1000

Young Leif is now back in Greenland, full of new ideas from Norway including a new religion – the Christian faith. He says it was taken there by missionary priests from Germany. Leif tries to encourage his family to become Christians, but Erik the Red is not willing. He's trusted the old Viking gods all his life, and feels it would be dangerous to desert them. Leif's mother wants Erik to build a Christian church. He's not happy!

In AD 922, Ibn Fadlan, a Muslim traveller in Russia, described how Viking merchants he met there said prayers to tall wooden statues of their gods.

Odin was the most powerful Viking god, the wisest, and the most mysterious. He was master of magic, poetry, runes (Viking writing) – but also of battles and madness.

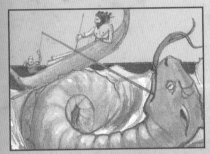

Thor, god of thunder, was big, brave, bold, strong, kindly, hot-tempered and stupid. He protected Viking farmers and craftsmen, and fought against monsters, such as the fearsome World-Serpent.

Loki was a spiteful trickster. who was clever, cunning and malicious. Neither gods nor people could trust him. He gave birth to magic animals, including Odin's eight-legged flying horse, Sleipnir.

The Norns were three veiled goddesses representing past, present and future. Sitting under Yggdrasil, the holy tree that supported the world, they measured out the threads of life and death for all humans.

Baldur was young and handsome. The other gods loved him and tried to protect him. But evil Loki killed him by a trick – using a sprig of magic mistletoe.

Frigg was the wife of Odin. She was clever and thoughtful. She spent her days spinning airy threads to weave into clouds.

Frey (right) and his sister **Freya** brought new life and love. They gave families many children. They sent rain and sunshine to make farm crops grow.

The Valkyries were wild female warrior-spirits. They flew over battlefields to carry back dead heroes to feast and fight in Odin's palace, Valhalla (the Hall of the Dead).

LAND! LAND!

Bjarni Herjolfsson's description of the new land he had seen caused excitement among the Greenland settlers. They had already bravely dared to leave their homes and sail west to settle in an unknown land. Now, many seemed keen to risk another adventure. Bjarni's new land might be better than Greenland.

AROUND AD 1000

I hear that young Leif has set off on another long voyage. He sailed away several weeks ago – into the unknown! This is no ordinary sailing trip to Iceland or Norway. I'm told that Leif bought Bjarni Herjolfsson's ship from him – and set off to find the mysterious land that Bjarni had glimpsed in the storm! He was last seen sailing north-west from Greenland. He's either a fool or a hero. Only time will tell!

Traders, raiders and explorers all planned their voyages carefully. After choosing a crew – around 35 men – they loaded their ship with all they might need for the voyage. Food, drink, spare sails and oars, and weapons were all essential. Viking ships might also carry trade goods, farm animals, soldiers or settler women and children.

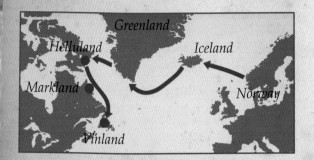

Leif and his men sailed north-west from Greenland and landed at Helluland (now Baffin Island), then at Markland (now Labrador). Both were bleak, cold and disappointing. So they headed south along the American coast and arrived at Vinland (now Newfoundland).

Traditionally, Viking settlers took carved timbers from the 'high' (best) seat in their old home and threw them overboard when they neared land. They would build their first new shelter where the timbers landed on shore.

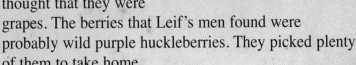

'Vinland' means 'Wineland'. Leif chose this name for his settlement in America after one of his men found juicy berries growing there, and thought that they were grapes. The berries that Leif's men found were probably wild purple huckleberries. They picked plenty of them to take home.

Leif's men met no-one in America. But Vikings who travelled there later traded with Native American people. They bartered (swapped) red Viking cloth for animal skins and furs.

Vikings called the American traders 'Skraelings'. They were probably members of the Beothuk First Nation, who lived by hunting and fishing.

VOYAGE TO THE WEST

In calm weather, and without maps or compasses to guide them, it was difficult for Leif and his crew to know whether they were following the same route as Bjarni. It took great courage to head out across the stormy Atlantic Ocean, not knowing what delights or dangers lay in store beyond the horizon.

...p, the
...e sharpest
...t lookout
...d and for
...ch as
...rocks, that
...k the ship
...its crew.

UNSUITABLE!
Helluland and Markland, the first places in North America where Leif landed, proved to be unsuitable sites for new settlements. At Helluland, the Vikings found nothing but huge slabs of rock. At Markland, there were trees for timber, but the weather was too wet, cold and foggy to ripen crops or raise farm animals. The further Leif's men sailed, the more eager and urgent their search became. Did they have doubts? We don't know. But some probably wondered if they would survive this adventure, and see their families and farms again.

Some Vikings may have used a kind of sundial as an aid to navigation.

LEIF THE LUCKY

After spending one winter in Vinland, Leif decided to sail back home. In spring, he loaded his boat with furs – and berries – and steered north-east, towards Greenland. But before he reached dry land, Leif had another adventure, which earned him a new nickname: 'Leif the Lucky'!

AROUND AD 1001

Land ahoy! Greenland is in sight! But on the little skerry (island) by the rocks Leif sees men – weak, but waving frantically. Leif rescues the shipwrecked sailors and in return they give him all their treasure!

Leif is welcomed home, but finds winter there has been very harsh. It's been bitterly cold, food is scarce, and many have died from sickness. Even Erik the Red has gone! Leif's brother Thorvald wants to go to Vinland straight away!

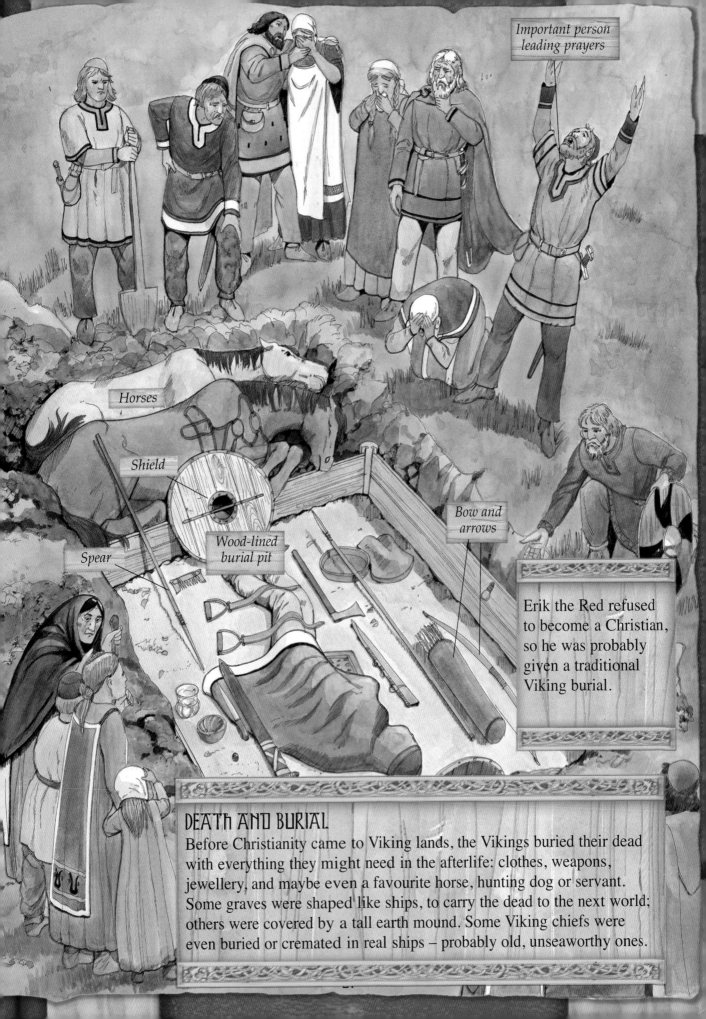

Important person
leading prayers

Horses

Shield

Spear

Wood-lined
burial pit

Bow and
arrows

Erik the Red refused
to become a Christian,
so he was probably
given a traditional
Viking burial.

DEATH AND BURIAL

Before Christianity came to Viking lands, the Vikings buried their dead
with everything they might need in the afterlife: clothes, weapons,
jewellery, and maybe even a favourite horse, hunting dog or servant.
Some graves were shaped like ships, to carry the dead to the next world;
others were covered by a tall earth mound. Some Viking chiefs were
even buried or cremated in real ships – probably old, unseaworthy ones.

NO RETURN!

Vikings who later sailed to America hoped to get rich by claiming land and trading, but none of them stayed there for long. The first to sail was Leif's brother, Thorvald, around AD 1005. Then, about five years later, Thorfinn Karlsefni, a Viking trader from Norway, set off for Vinland with sixty men, five women, and a herd of cattle. He was quickly followed by Freydis, Leif's sister, who led two ships full of settlers.

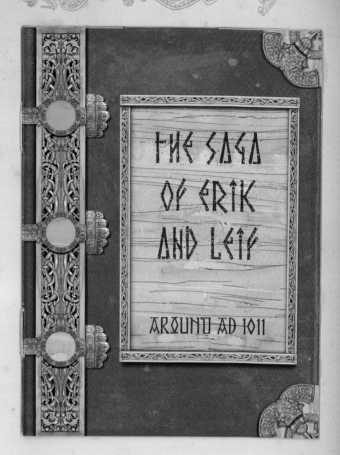

THE SAGA OF ERIK AND LEIF

AROUND AD 1011

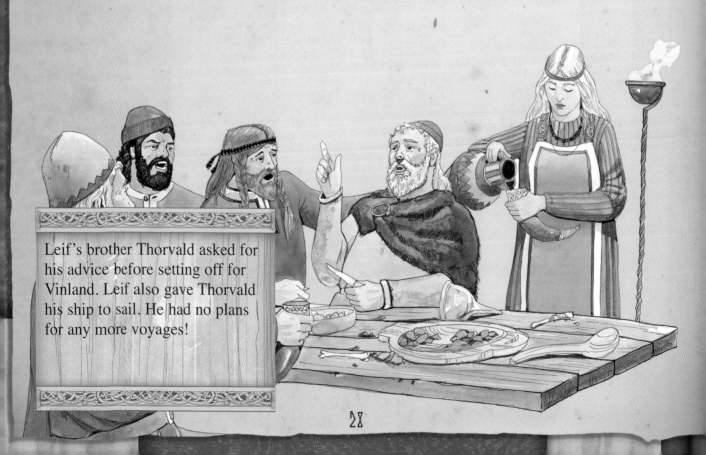

Leif's brother Thorvald asked for his advice before setting off for Vinland. Leif also gave Thorvald his ship to sail. He had no plans for any more voyages!

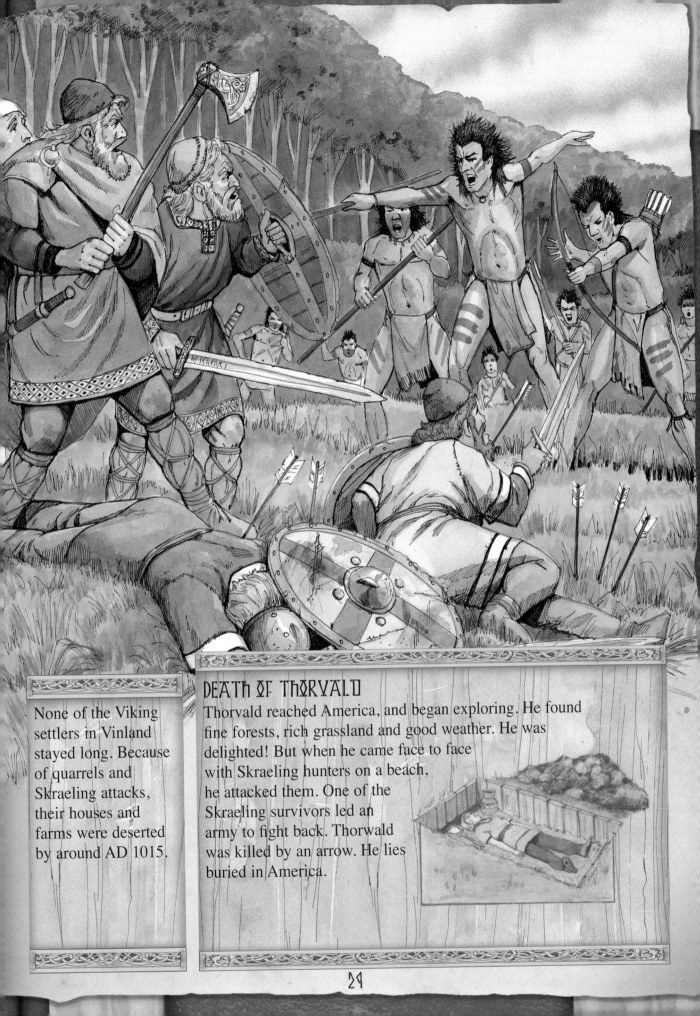

None of the Viking settlers in Vinland stayed long. Because of quarrels and Skraeling attacks, their houses and farms were deserted by around AD 1015.

DEATH OF THORVALD

Thorvald reached America, and began exploring. He found fine forests, rich grassland and good weather. He was delighted! But when he came face to face with Skraeling hunters on a beach, he attacked them. One of the Skraeling survivors led an army to fight back. Thorwald was killed by an arrow. He lies buried in America.

LASTING FAME

Leif Eriksson spent the rest of his life on his farm in Greenland, enjoying his memories – and his treasure.

AROUND AD 1020

Just like his father, Leif the Lucky has settled down on dry land. He has no wish to go sailing again or have great adventures. He does not know that he was the first European to land in the vast continent of America. And, unknown to him, the Viking settlements in Greenland will disappear, like his Vinland house, by around AD 1400. Perhaps he still wonders what other lands lie over the ocean, waiting to be explored?

Viking pin and spindle-whorl

Native American arrowhead

VIKING REMAINS

In 1961 archaeologists discovered the remains of eight Viking houses and a smithy at L'Anse aux Meadows, Newfoundland. Possibly they were built by Viking trader Thorfinn Karlsefni, around AD 1010. They also found a dress-pin and a spindle-whorl (a weight used in spinning thread) that once belonged to a Viking woman. A stone arrowhead found in Greenland shows that Native American hunters travelled east around the same time as the Vikings were voyaging west.

The saga (history) of Viking settlers in Iceland and Greenland was first written down around AD 1200. At least three different versions survive. About 50 years later, Erik and Leif's story was preserved in two entertaining epics: *The Saga of the Greenlanders* and *The Saga of Erik the Red*.

Thanks to the marvellous memories of skilful storytellers, the exciting adventures of Erik the Red and Leif the Lucky survived without being written down for over 200 years.

USEFUL WORDS

adze an axe-like tool used for smoothing and shaping wood.

amulet a charm, sometimes a gemstone, which is said to protect the wearer from harm.

barren unsuitable for growing crops or grazing cattle.

coax to convince by using a good argument.

distaff a thin wooden pole, used in spinning wool or flax, to keep the fibres from tangling.

earl a noble chieftain or war leader.

excavation the process of digging up historical artefacts and remains.

feud a long-standing argument between two groups or families, often leading to violence.

freeman a person who is not a slave, but also not a noble.

hearth a stone-lined fireplace used for cooking and heating.

hull the main body of a ship.

keel a large wooden beam, around which the hull of a ship is built.

knarr a merchant ship with a deep, wide hull.

landholding the right to own an unclaimed piece of land.

Law Speaker a wise man who recites the laws to ensure that people remember them.

longship a warship designed for speed.

noble a person from an important family.

outlaw a person who has been banished from a community for committing crimes.

peat the remains of long-dead plants, dug up from the ground. It can be used as a building material or as a fuel.

Pole Star a star that lies directly overhead when viewed from the North Pole.

runes Viking writing; some other civilisations used similar symbols.

saga a long story, often describing a person's entire life.

Scandanavia a large region covering present-day Sweden, Denmark and Norway; sometimes the name is also used to include Finland, Iceland, Greenland and neighbouring islands.

skald a Viking poet.

skerry a small, rocky island, too small to live on.

Skraelings the Viking name for the inhabitants of 'Vinland' (present-day Newfoundland), who traded with the Vikings.

smithy the workplace of a blacksmith.

stern the back end of a ship.

strake a curved wooden plank which forms part of the hull of a ship.

Thing a two-week-long meeting, occurring every summer, at which laws were recited and criminals punished.

Valhalla the Hall of the Dead, in the god Odin's palace, where Vikings believed their heroes were taken after death.

World-Serpent the snake which the Vikings believed surrounded the Earth, grasping its own tail.

Yggdrasil the World Tree, a great ash tree located at the centre of the universe, according to Viking beliefs.

INDEX

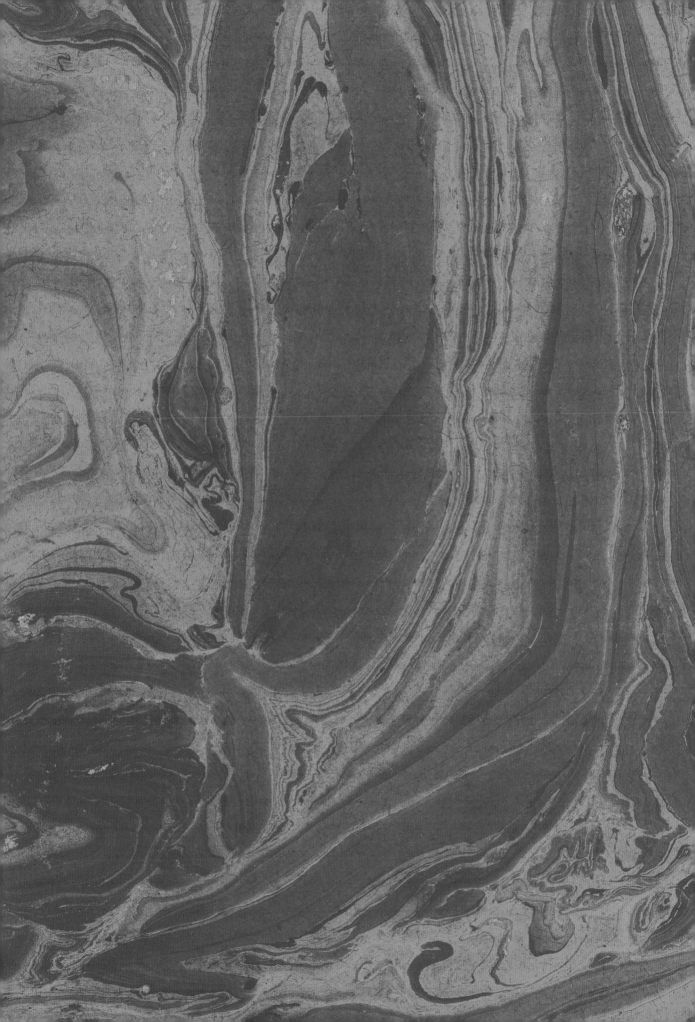

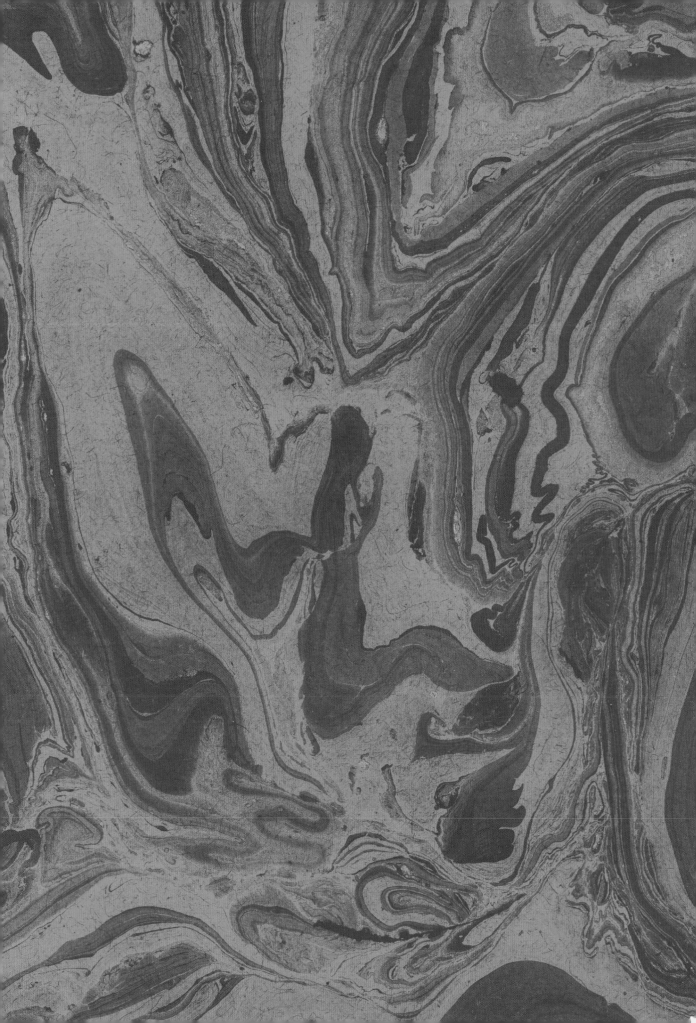